T0120969

I Rise
— to —
Inspire

Inspirational poems & Short stories for everyday living

OLIVIA ANSA-SAM GAVUA

authorHOUSE®

AuthorHouse™
1663 Liberty Drive
Bloomington, IN 47403
www.authorhouse.com
Phone: 1 (800) 839-8640

© 2018 Olivia Ansa-Sam Gavua. All rights reserved.

No part of this book may be reproduced, stored in a retrieval system, or transmitted by any means without the written permission of the author.

Published by AuthorHouse 02/15/2018

ISBN: 978-1-5462-2666-6 (sc)
ISBN: 978-1-5462-2665-9 (e)

Library of Congress Control Number: 2018901281

Print information available on the last page.

Any people depicted in stock imagery provided by Thinkstock are models, and such images are being used for illustrative purposes only. Certain stock imagery © Thinkstock.

This book is printed on acid-free paper.

Because of the dynamic nature of the Internet, any web addresses or links contained in this book may have changed since publication and may no longer be valid. The views expressed in this work are solely those of the author and do not necessarily reflect the views of the publisher, and the publisher hereby disclaims any responsibility for them.

Contents

Introduction

The book "I Rise to inspire' is a collection of poems that focus on themes related to love/Marriage, Perseverance, Faith/uplifting, Women, Men, children and friendship. The author finds these themes relevant to our times and generations to come and thus draws on her life experiences and many others to inspire and motivate her readers. The poems mainly constitute stories, songs, experiences, journey, and music of our life, which the author unleashes through creative verses to inspire readers to persevere and never relinquish to the inevitable storms of life.

The Poems on love / Marriage are compelling in the sense that they vividly capture and bring to the fore the core underpinnings of love such as eternity of love, the essential need for love by all humans, romance and standing firm to the complexities of love. The verses therefore challenge readers to arise and love unconditionally even in the midst of unexpected challenges and numerous unbearable situations that life presents to us.

Along the theme of perseverance, the author displays her creativity in writing by carefully choosing a diction that strongly energizes the reader to persevere in every aspect of their life. To this end the author, through her emphasis on perseverance does not only succeed in leaving a lasting impression on the minds of readers that there is a staying power in every soul but also forcefully drives home the point that success is indeed the hallmark of perseverance. The theme on perseverance also seeks to imbibe in readers a strong sense of encouragement. Under this same theme of perseverance, the author also confronts readers with this sudden urge and conviction not to be content with mediocrity but strive hard to break off from every limitation and transcend every negative situation that comes their way.

The author also employs the themes of faith and upliftment, which she utilizes to remind readers of the existence of a supreme power who is able to turn all negative situations around when called upon. As readers read the poems on faith, they are ushered into the poet's world of belief in God and are beaconed to call on and believe in this supreme power in times of hardships.

Furthermore, this collection of poems is well crafted to motivate Men, Women and Children to discover their unique potentials and roles in society and as readers get to the middle of the book they are inspired enough to want to do more and answer to the call of duty in society when called on.

Another fundamental pillar this book "I rise to inspire" seeks to immortalize is the sanctity of relationships. The author consciously impresses upon readers the need to adore beautiful friendships and relationships and constantly highlights the importance of loyalty in friendships as well as the essential roles friends play in our lives.

The verses in "I RISE TO INSPIRE" have a touch of humor. The author employs a lot of humor to put readers in a relaxation mode. There is no gainsaying this book will make one smile, laugh and even cry. Finally, the poems exude a strong sense of personalization. They will give you an urge to forge on without considering the least thought of throwing in the towel because they are your stories, your Journey and your songs. Readers without doubt will appreciate and enjoy these poems till the last page.

As the author of this book, I promise you this book will come in handy in times of hardships when you need an encouraging word to uplift and cheer you up. This book will be a lifetime inspiration to many generations.

Dedication

This Book is dedicated to my dear father Christopher Ansa-Sam Sr. of blessed memory who instilled in me the will power to attain and achieve anything I want in life. Daddy, you will forever be appreciated.

To my mother Susana Ansa-Sam. Thanks for all the sacrifices you made for me to be whom I am today. You sacrificed more than any human being could sacrifice for me. Each day, I am encouraged to forge on in life because of the strength I draw from you. I am a strong woman because you taught me how to fight without given up.

Acknowledgement

I never had any intentions of writing or publishing an inspirational poetry book. I enjoy writing and as I put together my experiences and life lessons in words, I shared them with my family and friends. I was astounded by their reactions. My friends and family exhumed in me a talent I didn't know I had. As I kept sharing my inspirational poems, these friends gave me more confidence to keep writing. They consistently told me how the poems had inspired them to persevere and how each poem left a glimmer of hope and a smile on their faces.

I would like to thank my wonderful and supportive husband Eric Gavua who always believed in me and cheered me on even when I didn't believe in myself. Eric, I really appreciate your resolute support and constant encouragement to keep writing this book. Thanks for taking time to read and listen to my poems every evening. I know you were too tired and sleepy to listen to me recite each poem I wrote, but you grappled to stay awake to listen just to make me happy. Trust me, I know they were annoying sometimes but you endured it. Thank you very much, you are very much appreciated and I couldn't have done it without you.

To my dear friend Angela Adofo, I can never thank you enough for the confidence you built in me. It all started with a poem I wrote for you on your birthday. Thanks for cheering me on, one poem at a time.

I would like to express my utmost gratitude to my dear brother Ernest Ansah-Sam who took time to read my poems and encourage me to publish my book. I could never have done it without your encouraging and motivational push.

To my Sister in- Law, Rosemond Mansa Bordzoe, I have nothing but deep appreciation for taking time to read my poems and for constantly reminding me to share my talent of creative writing. Thanks for all the insightful comments.

Furthermore, I would like to thank my co-workers and friends Yvette Jackson-Fains and Vicky Rice for the confidence you gave me after reading each poem. You were part of the reason why I continued writing. Each week you asked for a new poem because my poem brought smiles to your faces and that was what kept me writing. Thank you!

Last but not the least, I am very grateful to Eryka Gavua, Aaron Gavua and my siblings Emmanuel Ansa-Sam and Dorothy Manful for supporting me with your prayers. God Bless you all.

Foreword

The expression of thought, creativity, style and language constitutes one of the central aims of poetry. Poetry is also considered as a powerful conduit that connects our imagination to the land of ideas and creativity. It provides the outlet to express our human emotions as well. As a trained academic who is actively involved in the required academic undertakings for a living, I can say that I enjoy what I do, but my lifelong interest in poetry has not escaped my personal orbit. I love to read and listen to poetry for inspiration!

The title of this new collection, "I Rise to Inspire" by Olivia Ansa-Sam is not only important and relevant to me and many others who will read this inspirational poetry, but this brilliant piece of work is timely in our contemporary era where strong and inspirational voices are needed. Poet Ansa-Sam is indeed one of the inspirational voices of our times who is bringing the language of encouragement, love, friendship, forgiveness and hope into our lives and spaces through this excellent book. I have known Olivia and her family for many years. Not only is her commitment to the field of poetry very profound, but I have always been impressed by how Olivia integrates her strong educational background with her knowledge, poetic skills and experiences of life to write inspirational poems that connect to the heart of the human condition.

This collection of poetry is a great masterpiece that tells extraordinary and courageous stories with creativity and elegance. The poems cover interesting and relevant areas of faith, love, marriage, friendship, forgiveness, perseverance and other areas that pertain to life in general. Reading these poems will definitely inspire and challenge you in many positive ways. Your love for poetry would also be enhanced in many dimensions. For example, the poem, "The Loud Silence" highlights the unique complexity and style of Olivia in terms of her originality in crafting poetic language and terms such as "loud and silence" at the same time. This epitomizes the excellent and well-written poems you would find in this book. This collection of published works is certainly a must read for all. Enjoy reading these inspirational poems by Olivia Ansa-Sam.

Felix Kumah-Abiwu, Ph.D.
Assistant Professor of African Affairs
Kent State University

Foreword

We have heard it said several times that "music makes the world go round". I consider poetry as a form of music which has the power to inform us, draw us into places seen and unseen, encourage, soothe, and challenge us to keep persevering in the daily struggles and joys of life. Writing of any kind is not an easy task. For those who write out of the joy of writing or for those who write out of necessity—as a job, writing can be a daunting task. I have often wondered about poets, who not only write like most writers do, but write in various ways that speak to different people through the power of the pen.

Poetry goes beyond words written on a piece of paper. Indeed, good poetry has the power to take the reader on a journey that simply requires one's imagination as a passport to experience all the different senses of the body. Poems invite us into the mind and soul of the writer as we experience and share in the humanity that engulfs them as they pour out their minds and hearts through words.

The work of the poet takes many skills. It is a combination of artistic capabilities and mastery over imagery, words and style to produce poems that speak to our senses. I have often wondered how poets write words and draw imagery that speak so clearly and closely to one's state of mind and makes you marvel at their skill and candor.

The poems in this collection are drawn from the innermost being of the poet. Combining her passion for poetry and love of inspiring people around her, the poet draws us into her world through words and images that seek to inspire us in love and in faith. The poems in this collection speak to the family unit as a whole, starting with poems that inspire love and marriage. Through words that invoke the memories of a loved one both distant and near, we catch various glimpses of what we can each aspire for in our relationships. The poems also speak to children in the family and invite us to reflect on friendship.

Through the great works of female poets like Ama Ata Aidoo, one can begin to see the birth of a new generation of poets whose works will continue to inspire and speak to us for years to come. I hope you will find in this collection poems that speak to you, poems that inspire you and poems that you can share with your friends and loved ones. If music makes the world go round, poetry is the wheel that turns the world round. May you find in this collection words that turn your world around.

Josephine Jarpa Dawuni Ph.D – Assistant Professor – Howard University

Foreword

This eclectic yet interconnected book of poems highlights the rudiments of love and human existential contingencies in its ephemeral and elongated impactful sense. It conveys the essence of love with meaning as demonstrated by intentionally explicit and implicit communicative rationality, action and/or otherwise in ways that denote health and general wellbeing of committed souls. The unique and related themes of love, passionate patience, resilience, acceptance, forgiveness, warm friendliness, alert discipline, faith in the human spirit, vocation, joy, disruption, family, intersection of tradition and modernity, and divinity among others enable the reader to appreciate the lived reality of conjugal union and its intended and unintended societal expectations with the commonweal as the overriding telos.

The readers will certainly admire Olivia Ansa-Sam's (author) interpretive approach in relating thematic essentials regarding the truth about human union/relationships with attendant universal and relative situations regardless of the locale. The book enriches the soul, heightens the beauty of unconditional love, fosters acceptance of unavoidable realities, emboldens the experienced and gives hope to the up-and-coming. The book unequivocally adds value to its reader notwithstanding the age bracket and conveys the connectedness and inextricable intergenerational existential yet divinely ordained human engagements and interactions with the authentic self at its core.

Dr. James K. Agbodzakey, Associate Professor and author of *Every Soul Counts: A Manual for Christian Growth*

Love/Marriage

Broken Together

"Let's stay broken together"
He pleads with her,
This journey has been long and unpredictable,
Though predictable from the beginning
When we said "we do".
Strong and untainted was our love,
Our love, now tainted by our imperfections and
disappointments.
Our imperfections have brewed anger, impatience and
ailments
Though the future looks bleak and unpredictable
There is one thing I know "our love is remediable.

"Let's stay broken together"
He pleads with her.
Just like a guest doesn't stay long, let's treat anger like a
guest
And empathy as a member of our family
Remember love is like hot water; it boils rapidly and
cools down after a while
When we are broken and our love has cooled down,
don't walk away,
Let's stay broken together

Because in the eyes of God we are malleable
And he is able to mold us over again
Or perhaps we are imperfect
And our inherent imperfections keeps us together
Though broken, we complement each other -
So "let's stay broken together" he pleads with her.

Stood Together

When it was raining hard
We held hands and stood together
Some days we were lucky-
Lucky to have one broken umbrella,
And we stood together under that broken umbrella.
When the waters were rising high
He would carry me because he was taller
And was lucky enough to rise above the rising waters
He would carry me, so I wouldn't drown
When the temperatures were too cold
We stood
We stood together
And wrapped ourselves with the only tattered blanket
we had.
When the earthly judges kept saying "no, you can't"
We stood together and said "yes, we can".
When we had just one ladle of rice to eat for dinner,
We shared.
When the giants rose to fight us
We stood and slung our five stones at the giants.
Today, we are still standing because we stood.
We stood the test of time and the changing scenes of life
Because we stood together.
There is power in standing together!

The Loud Silence

The Loud silence
The silence is so loud
So loud it keeps me awake.
I hear the silence screaming
"You, you are alone and lonely forever"
The loud silence around me scares me
And I ask myself, will I be lonely forever?
As I lay in the comfort of my bed,
I yearn for the touch of a lover
A lover who will caress and hold me tight
A lover who would block my ears with his tongue
Till I can't hear the loud silence anymore

My soul aches for a lover who would give me a baby
A baby who would cry so loud-
So loud till I can't hear the loud silence anymore
I have searched and looked everywhere
Travelled around the world to find that lover
But to no avail
Sometimes I cry in my dreams
Because the loud silence is so prevalent in my dreams
Oh Lord! I am calling unto you, give me a lover and a baby!
Who would block and take away this **loud silence.**

Mr Music Man

Mr. Music Man
Your Music makes me want to sing all day
And dance all night
Mr. Music man
Your music tingles my ears and creates a beat in my soul
That music is so sick; it makes me want to kick off my heels
When those heels are off-
I will rumba and samba till those hips are dislocated
When those hips are dislocated, my intense pleasure will be
located.
Mr. Music Man, don't stop that music, play on!
Let your music lead me to the place where I find ardent
healing
Mr. Music Man, let your music keep my ageing brain alert
to its ceiling.
Oh! How I love to hear you play that music
When your music stops, the expression of humanity stops.
Humanity! Express yourself to that beat
Defeat the cares and burdens of this world with that beat.
Let Mr. Music Man take you to a place of serenity and
self-identity
Mr. Music Man, play on! The world is listening and
dancing.

Marriage/Love

10 Days

I didn't realize how much space he had occupied in my life
Till he was gone for ten days
Twelve years, he held my hands every night till we fell asleep
Twelve years, I had a story to tell him every day after work
And he listened without flinching
Twelve years he laughed at my silly jokes
And made me feel like I was the source of his joy on earth
Twelve years he listened to me vent when I was upset about anything
And made me feel better
But when he was gone for 10 days
I came home every day and didn't have anybody to tell my stories
10 days, I looked for that hand to hold at night
And there was no hand
I opened my hands wide and cried myself to sleep
When he was gone for ten days, I had nobody to listen to my silly jokes
The jokes kept building up
And the emptiness kept piling up
Ten days, certainly confirmed my feelings and doubts I had had for 12years
This man had irrefutably taken a special place in my life that couldn't be filled-
Filled by my kids or anyone else
Ten days, I would forever hold him tight

Pen pals

Pen Pals that is all we were
Or so I thought we were
"There is power in the pen" they say
Indeed the pen is like a sharp tongue
My Pen Pal,
We had never met
But it was as though he was my guardian angel
We bonded through a pen
He was always there to comfort me with his pen
I shared my sad moments with him
And he listened on paper
I shared my worries with him
And he listened on paper
My Pen pal,
He wooed me with his pen
Till we fell in love
He was miles away but I could feel his hug through his
letters
He is my husband now
And he is still my pen pal
Because he still writes me love letters every day with his pen
He is still winning with his pen
Because he's won my heart forever
He will be my pen Pal till death do us part!

She Sowed Bountifully
She Reaped Bountifully

Each Morning he woke up
He Laid by her
And gazed undistracted at her face while she was in deep
 slumber
Each morning he would ponder
On what he could do to make her happy
She on the other hand
Had been dropping seeds of love in his heart at night
While he was in deep slumber
The seeds of love will blossom
Every morning while he was awake
She loved hard
He loved harder
She jumped hurdles to attain his love
He jumped leaps of fences to sustain her love
She treated him as though
He was the king of Zamunda
And he called her his queen

She forgave him each time he erred
And he never saw her flaws
She gave him the freedom to be himself
He couldn't stay away for too long
Without her
He spoiled her like a mistress
And he always had a beam on his face
Each day he said to her
"I love you so much"
And she responded
"My love for you is till eternity"
She sowed bountifully in him
She reaped bountifully
He gave her more than
He would give to the state of Maryland

Perseverance

She danced To the Tune

She heard the tune
It tingled her feet
She stood and began dancing
The tune was solemn
But the language was foreign
She did not understand the words
But she kept dancing
The music changed
This time the tune was faster
So she changed her style and her steps were electric
As she accelerated her steps, the dance became hectic
But she kept dancing
The tune changed again
Some dancers on the floor became indignant
And left when the tune changed
But she kept dancing to the tune
"The tune of life may change but don't stop dancing to
the Tune"
She yelled out to her fellow dancers.

While Waiting

I waited so long for this day
I waited tirelessly for this day
Some days I thought I would stray-
Stray from my faith
Some days I strayed from my goal
The wait was taking a toll
And I was beginning to lose control
Or perhaps I thought I was in control
While waiting I stressed and digressed
Human as I was, that was the only way
The wait was excruciating and frustrating
My strength was gradually diminishing

Then something happened
While Waiting
I began to count my blessings
And then I stopped stressing
I began to pray
Then I stopped straying
I regained my focus
Then came my bonus
The bonus of Joy and strength
While Waiting
Through it all I have learned to be patient and expectant
While Waiting

Stronger Than Yesterday

Impoverished parents bore him
Impoverished land he was born on
Poverty-stricken were his people
A wretched life he had to live

Life itself had broken his bones
Life had left indelible scars on him
He was never ashamed of his scars
Because they were signs of his inner strength
His indomitable spirit wouldn't let him stay broken
All his broken pieces he picked
And travelled to a land far away –
Far away where he could find greener pastures
His Journey to greener pastures
Would leave deeper wounds and more visible scars
But his past experience had made him stronger and resilient
His past experience had thought him to carry on-
Carry on, when he didn't have the strength to
His past experience had definitely made him stronger than
yesterday!

The Imprisoned Dolphin

In the deep blue waters
Where the tides rise and fall
The Dolphin, the smartest of them all
In the water kingdom
Splashes its pectoral fins, wags its smooth fluke
And leaps many lengths
Above the waters to display its intelligence
The dolphin flaunts its love for mankind
Fascinates mankind with its curiosity
And leaps above the waters
To reach the limitless skies
Human kind is bedazzled at its brilliance
But soon the dolphin will be imprisoned by the
dictators of the world.
The creators of boundaries and restrictions
Have succeeded for a moment
To restrict the leaps of the dolphin
For a moment the dolphin
Is unable to leap high out of the waters to get air

The dolphin is gasping for air-
Gasping for air to display its intelligence
Suddenly the dolphin is imprisoned
But it is only for a moment
Soon the imprisoned dolphin
Will navigate
Out of the waters
To higher leaps and bounds.
Soon the imprisoned Dolphin
Will be free to leap to higher heights

No Comfort Zones

She knows no comfort zones
Because to her the sky is the limit
She itches to fly high to the limitless skies
And indeed nothing can stop her
Nothing will stop her!
Her indomitable spirit will keep her persevering and
resisting-
Resisting all the negative forces
All the negative forces along the way, will be crushed!
All the hurdles will be crossed!
Because she is indefatigable

She can still hear the still small voice of her dad telling her-
"Do not be afraid to fly high, the sky is your limit"
She would not rest
Comfort Zones make her restless and breathless
She has to forge on to the ultimate
She will commit herself to her goals
Knowing that her achievement is definite
No comfort zones will be entertained till the sky is reached!

One Last Try

He went with all he had in his hands
Each time he went with all he had been given by God
Each time he gave his all
In his hands he had Faith,
In his hands he had skill and experience
In his hands he had brilliance and persistence
In his appearance and utterance you could see radiance
His substance had balance
He possessed a natural flow of eloquence
But the panelists could not see what he had in his hands
The earthly judges could not judge accurately
Because they lacked foresight

He kept his focus
And kept refocusing without swaying
He kept going and reappearing
And all he could hear from the earthly judges was "No"
All he could hear from the panelists was "No"
If only they knew what he had in his hands.
He was getting weary
And his resistance was becoming nonexistence
He had decided not to appear anymore
She on the other hand saw what he had
She persuaded him to give his one last try
And he did-He gave his **one last try**

With all he had in his hands
And suddenly the earthly judges could see
They could see radiance and brilliance

They could see excellence in his performance
Suddenly he had attained acceptance
That one last Try will change his life forever!

My Own Small Victory

I quivered when I received the call
But I answered the call
I answered the call with ambiguity
But I spoke with certainty
The lady on the other side of the call
Concluded I was perspicacious
And that was my own small victory

I quivered when I was called in for a meeting
But I answered the call
At the meeting, I was weak within
But was brave enough to face my fears
I faced my fears
Because I didn't have what was required
But the lady on the other side
Was impressed with what I had to say
And that was my own small victory

I quivered when I was asked to join them
I didn't have what was required
But I answered the call
And appeared on the day of reckoning

They were impressed
But deep within me I was petrified
Because I didn't have what was required
I quivered when I was asked to provide what I had
But I answered the call
And provided what I had
It was all I had, but it wasn't what they required
I couldn't join them
But I answered the call
And faced my fears of rejection
I learned a lesson.
I walked out very proud and unbending
I had conquered my fears
And that was my own small victory

Uplifting/Faith/ Spiritual

What I Know

Many things I know
But this I know for sure
I know that if I knock hard and long enough
Someone will hear and open the door
Many things I know
But this I know for sure
If I ask, though it may tarry
I will surely receive it someday
Many things I know
But this I know for sure
Worry and faith
Cannot reside in the mind at the same time
Many things I know
But this I know for sure
If I can't stop thinking about it
I must put into action and it will become a reality
Many things I know
But this I know for sure
I know that no situation is permanent
Nothing exists longer than an instant
Except the memories we hold so dearly
Many things I know
But this I know for sure
I know that life is too short
To take the people we love for granted
Live every moment to the fullest and let your light shine
In every moment
These are the things I know, for sure!

The Question Is

The question is-
Why do you feel unaccepted?
When you have an impactful sign on your forehead
That yells "accepted"
The Question is -
Why do you worry about tomorrow?
When tomorrow is not guaranteed
The Question is –
Why are you waiting for opportunity to knock?
When you have no door
The Question is –
Why do you expect so much?
When you've done nothing, with what you've been given.
The Question is –
Why are you so quick to judge?
When you haven't swept your own front door
The Question is –
How many steps have you taken to reach your Canaan?

The Question Is –
Why are you finding yourself?
When you haven't created yourself
The question is –
Why do you expect life to love you?
When you haven't loved life

The question is –
Why do you anticipate a positive outcome?
When you've only contemplated on the negative
The Question is-
Why do you feel conquered?
When your creator has made you a conqueror
The Question is –
What have you done for others today?
When you have been endowed with so much

Honorably Imperfect

I, honorably imperfect
In every aspect
Having learned to accept my imperfections
Was the smartest acceptance I would make
Though long coming
It was quite stunning
When I reached that realization-
A realization that brought a sensation
A sensation that brought an urge-
To strive for perfection
Today I say
 I am not afraid of perfection
Today I say
I will unapologetically be myself
I am honorably imperfect
And accept all others as honorably imperfect

The Ubiquitous Onlooker

The Ubiquitous Onlooker
He is everywhere
He can't be seen anywhere
Yet his presence is everywhere
He is invisible but very invincible
His ubiquitous presence is inexplicable
He cannot be seen but many call on him
Because they feel his strong presence
And know he hears when they call

The Ubiquitous Onlooker
He has many names
Sometimes we don't feel his presence
Because he acts oblivious when the storms of life roar
But the Ubiquitous onlooker is right there
Watching, looking and observing as you grow in the
midst of the storm
When the storm is unsurmountable he steps in
In he steps, he takes over and he calms down the storm
When he takes over there is no need to panic
Because he is the ubiquitous on looker!

Learning to sail my ship

It was the dawn of a beautiful day
As I sat in my beautifully adorned ship
Handed over to me by my creator
My ship rocked to and fro
I had no idea
How to sail my ship
I had no idea
How to navigate my ship
In the direction I wanted it to go
My ship was in the middle
Of a deep and wide Ocean
With many other ships ahead of me
Most sailors had massive experience
I had minimal experience
Some days the storms were as calm
As death
Some days the storms were as rough
As a grater
Some days the storms were cruel
But I was learning to sail my ship
I sailed like a snail
While others sailed like birds
Some days it felt
As though I would sink
But I wasn't afraid to sink
I battled with what to do next

Because I was learning to sail my ship
I found out
It may take years to arrive at the shore
Some days I may digress
Some days I may feel like
Stopping in the middle of the Ocean
But I wouldn't stop-
Learning to sail my ship
I will keep sailing
Someday I will arrive at the shore.

A Citizen of Faith

I, a citizen of faith
As cliché as it may sound
I am a citizen of faith
In the land of faith
Flows honey and milk
In the land of faith
Problems are temporary like a set
And miracles grow like plants
I, a citizen of faith
Wear patience as my armor
And prayer as my sword
I am a citizen of faith
And cannot befriend a citizen of worry
Because worry is a foe
And it is impossible for us to co-exist
In the land of faith
Dreams are born by the minute
Dreams grow like plants
Dreams become a reality
I am a citizen of faith
And I choose to believe in the unforeseen

Changing Scenes

Changing Scenes
I have seen the Scenes change so many times
Like an unfolding story in a play
The scenes change overtime
Some of the scenes are mirthful to watch
Some very sorrowful to watch
Scenes, they are like seasons, they are not permanent-
Sometimes they are cold
Sometimes warm
Changing Scenes, it constantly puts me in a state of
incredulity

But I always bounce back with a smile
Because I am like an actor
Taking cues from my maker
Who is also the master of the scenes
Changing Scenes! Is what I call life
Every Scene comes with its own lesson
I have learned to stay calm when the scenes change
With each changing scene, I will indulge the pleasures and
woes-
Knowing that there is a master who oversees the scenes when
it is at its climax
The Changing Scenes, will be mutable till the end of time.

The Glorious Unfolding

Stand Up! Wake Up!
Do you see a glorious unfolding coming?
Do you hear a glorious unfolding knocking?
Sometimes it awakes me in the morning
With a strong urge to fight on
It purges all my worries,
The glorious unfolding gives me hope
That hope gives me a persevering spirit
A persevering spirit that is so indomitable, so
unstoppable and unconquerable
I will smile through the challenges
And sometimes I will cry
But I will quickly wipe away the tears,
Because I know there is a glorious unfolding coming
and I will live to see it.

The Beginning of an End

The beautiful robin chirps
The cock crows
Scents of fried bacon in the air
I am startled
By the chirping
I am startled
By the scents of fried bacon
It is a sign of a new day
It is a sign of an awakening -
An awakening
To a new day of continuous struggle
A new day of continuous misfortune
I am bombarded by ill luck
I am bombarded by blockages
Nowhere to run to
No body to talk to
The sun has gone down on me
The sun has refused to shine
The sun is Oblivious to the chirping of the robins
It is darkness all around me
Has my very existence caused the sun not to shine?
Caused the sun not to shine?

As I lay my troubling soul to rest
I fall into a deep slumber
Sleeping like a log
But suddenly I hear

The robin chirp
This time the chirping
Is different, it is a new sound
It is a new robin
A colorful robin
Suddenly I hear the cock crow
The crow is different
This time it is a new cock
A colorful cock
And I hear the robin chirp
"It is the beginning of an ending"
And I hear the cock crow
"It is the beginning of an end"
The bacon smells different
Suddenly I am awakened
To the beginning of an end.

Forgiveness

I forgive because I give
When I forgive
I give to myself good health and a happy spirit
If I don't forgive then I'm spiritless
I forgive because it is right for my soul
And forgiveness is needed for every soul
Arise my brother! Arise my sister!
Do you hear the bells of forgiveness ringing?
It is calling on you to forgive,
Forgiveness is giving and freeing
And your soul yearns for that freedom
Forgiveness returns blessings
And blessings are needed by many
Give! Give the gift of forgiveness!
Because it is right to forgive

Mr. Preacher Man

While you stood in the pulpit
You touched the heart of the culprit
As you delivered your message of truth
You touched the heart of the man who shot the bullet
You spoke with such brilliance and eloquence
And brought the whole congregation to repentance
Mr. Preacher Man
To many, you walk your talk
To many, you meet the felt need of your congregation
As a man of integrity, you rise to every occasion
Your sacrificial attitude is greeted with a standing ovation
You are not a pulpiteer
You exalt Christ only
Because you have been called-
Called by your Lord to lead, love and to restore

Mr. Preacher Man
Preach that message I love to hear
That message of veracity-
Preach to me that message that brings me clarity
Preach to me that word of authenticity
Because that message frees me from all the cares and burdens
of this world
Mr. Preacher Man, let your divine message bring restoration
to all nations
Mr. Preacher Man, preach on! The world is listening and
conforming.

That Voice

I hanker for that voice
Because it is my first choice
My first choice in every decision
That voice gives me a vision
A vision of certainty
Certainty that the path I'm taking will be alright
Certainty that the path will be right
Sometimes it is arduous to hear that Voice
And I grapple with the pain of not hearing that Voice
Oh! Let me hear that voice distinctly!
Oh! Let me hear that voice patently!
Oh! I need to hear that voice perceptibly!

So Far so full of Praise

Behold our provider
Behold our protector
Behold our connector
Behold our up lifter
Unaccustomed to the fluidity of life
Yet accustomed to many hardships
That slapped the face
Like hard rain drops
You left your holy place
High above the earth
To be by our side
Behold our companion
Our burdens you carried
Our worries you weaned
Our fears you flushed-
Away
Our hearts you delighted
With Many blessings
Beyond human understanding

Today we say
You have made us story tellers
Today we say
So far we are so full of praise
When we rise.
Today, we say
So far, we are so full of praise
When we talk.
Today we say
We are so full of praise
When we lay our heads to rest
Today we say
Receive our hearts so full of praise!

Life Lessons

Laugh Out Loud

When he laughed out loud
Her feet tickled
When he laughed out loud
She laughed so hard
Her ribs felt brittle
Life had taught him
To laugh out loud
When he was frustrated
Life had taught him
To laugh out loud
When he was exhausted
Because laughter brought a surge of elation
That was commensurate to liberation
Life had taught him
To laugh out loud
Because it was a contagious sensation
That touched all nations
Life had taught him
To laugh out loud
Because laughter was a language understood by all races
Are you laughing out loud?
Laugh at life
Laugh out loud at your frustrations
Laugh out loud at the escalations
Laugh out loud at the cessations
Laugh out loud at the ovations
And never cease laughing out loud!

Be Careful

Oh! Be careful you who wears tattered clothes
    Be careful what your ears hear
Oh! You who wears tattered clothes, be careful
    Be careful what your eyes see
Oh! You who wears tattered clothes be careful
    Be careful what your mouth says
Oh! You who wears tattered clothes be careful
    Be careful how you play
Because your clothes might get ripped –
    Ripped while you play rough
And there will be none for you to wear
    So be careful
Be careful you who wears tattered clothes!

Unchanged lanes

She drove on that lane
She reflected on that lane.
For so many years
That lane was smooth
Void of any uncouth drivers.
There were no bumpy rides
The lane was comfortable
And she stayed with it.
For her, the lanes didn't change much
Because she was content
Many years,
She wondered what happened
In the other lanes
For many years
She yearned to know
What happened in the other lanes
She would never know
Because she never changed lanes

Mystery beyond Misery

Mystery beyond misery,
I would say it was quite slippery
The way he slipped through the hands of life
A beautiful afternoon it was at the beach
Where he was captivated by her curves and beauty
She walked to and fro, as if she was on duty
On duty to find something,
Something to take with her
He on the other hand, couldn't resist her
He followed her everywhere
He would go anywhere-
With her.
"Your beauty keeps calling my name" He said to her.
She said "Come! Ski with me"
Mystery beyond misery had begun unfolding.

Mystery beyond misery
Took a hold of the scenery
And everything became gloom
His peers watched, as he climbed behind her on the ski boat
She slipped and fell in the ocean
He jumped into the ocean, to save her from the woes of the ocean
But soon they would be swallowed by the woes of the ocean
They were gone, gone and never to be seen again
It was a mystery beyond Misery.

Women

Dedicated to all Women

Bending But Not Breaking

She bends; she bends and bends but does not break!
What is this woman made of?
She bends and bends but does not break!
Just like a bamboo tree she has withered the storms
The storms have blown her to and fro-
Twisting, bending, churning, turning and shaking the very
core of her existence
But she does not break,
Nor would she conform.
No! She would not conform to the realities of the storms.
She is like a tea bag; she would only become stronger –
Stronger only when she is in hot waters.
Her strength is immeasurable and inexorable!
With her unassuming strength she embraces her children
And watches over them like a hawk.
Sometimes she may look frail but she will prevail
Sometimes she may look as though she is breaking
But don't be deceived she would not break!
She would bend and bend and bend but she would not break
What is this woman made of?

Glitters of Doom

She turned the kind one down
She turned the nice one down
She was looking for glitters of gold
Or perhaps glitters of doom
She turned the short one down
She turned the tallest one down
She was looking for glitters of gold
Or perhaps glitters of doom
She turned the poor one down
She turned the hardworking man down
But he loved her with all his heart
What was she looking for?
She wanted it all, she wanted glitters of gold
Or perhaps glitters of doom
She finally found him, he glittered like gold
She thought he had it all
But all too soon she discovered
He was glitters of doom
She was stuck-
Stuck with glitters of doom
Who would rescue her?

Pretty Girl, Why Worry?

Oh pretty girl
Oh a beautiful soul thou possess
Oh your almond shaped eyes gaze deep into every soul
It enchants the wicked soul
Oh pretty girl you are
Your smile enraptures the cold hearted
Oh pretty girl you are
Your beautiful long legs
Are like the rod of Moses
When you step,
All the problems of mankind are resolved

Oh pretty girl
Why worry about the amazing man who will marry you?
Say a prayer to him
Who knows it all
You will see him
In dreams and in reality
Step out in style
Search for him
Hunt for him
And when you have found him
Examine him
You would know

He was the man in your dreams
Oh pretty girl you are
When you find him
He will tell you
How you've captivated his heart
He will tell you
How long he's been searching for you
He will hold you forever
And never let go
Oh pretty girl you are
Why worry about the man who will betroth you?

Oh Drama Girl

Oh drama girl
You declare you love pearls
But you belittle your girlfriend's pearls
Oh drama girl
You adore kiss curls
But you despise your girlfriend's curls
Oh! Drama girl
You love to twirl
But you secretly wish
Your girlfriend will twirl
Off the cliff
Oh drama girl
When will you stop bickering?
When will you stop gibbering?
When will you start seeing
Your girlfriend shine
Through the fog you've created
Oh! Drama girl
You say you hate drama
Yet you are the propeller of drama

Have you failed to realize
That a strong sisterhood builds-
A strong nation?
Oh Drama girl!
Wake up from your constant nonsensical demeanor!
Say no to girlfriend drama
Build a strong sisterhood
Build a strong motherhood
Enjoy your girlfriend
She is the only one who understands you
Oh! Drama girl
I hope you change your ways soon

She Spiced It Up

Don't waste my time lady
I've got things to spice up
Don't waste my time lady
I've got my love life to spice up
My lover awaits patiently
As if he has no cares in the world
He awaits complacently
Because when things are spiced up
All is luscious
And all is turned up
Don't waste my time lady
I've got things to spice up
I've got my outfits to spice up
Because I can get whatever I want
When I am all dolled up
Don't waste my time lady
I've got my cooking to spice up
Because that is the only way
To my lover's heart
Don't waste my time lady
I've got my mansion to spice up
Because my in-laws are visiting
And I need to enthrall them

Don't waste my time lady
I've got my work clothes to spice up
Because life is too short to wear boring clothes
Let me spice it up, lady!
Let me spice this moment up
Let me spice this life up
Because it is all I have
I get to live it once
And once is enough to spice it up.

The best dressed lady

As she walked into the room
Her face bloomed
Her dark skin
Like a dark Hershey chocolate, glowed
She bloomed like a rose tree
On a ruined wall
She was delightfully trimmed
She wore a lace fitting dress
That fit like a glove
Her metallic belt was as solid as an armor
And as sensual as a piece of Jewelry
Her high heels were pointy and on point
She walked in fashionably late
In a grand style
Her style was grand indeed
The room was dull
Till she walked in
All heads turned
As she walked in

Each time she surprised
The crowd with her lustrous looks
She was friendly with all the gentlemen
But she always had one nice gentleman
In her corner
Who completed her looks
He was her best accessory
He was the finishing touch
To her best dressed looks
But most important of all
Was her inner beauty
It radiated from deep within
Her radiant smile crowned it all
Her smile ultimately crowned her
The best dressed lady

Never to Remember

Erased from my mind
Never to remember
How badly you treated me
How you looked at me as though I was a worm
Never to remember how you scorned me
In the presence of my peers
As though I was the adulterous woman at the well
Erased from my mind
Never to remember how you trampled on me
Like a snake
Never to remember how you
Whispered demeaning words to bring me down
On the most meaningful day of my life
Never to remember how you detested to adore me
Erased from my mind
Never to remember how you ridiculed me like a clown
I would never remember
Because I am immensely loved and appreciated by someone
And I forgive and forget!

Men

Dedicated to all Men

Men of Valor

Men of Valor
They carry their badge with honor
With pride they honor the legacy handed over to them by
 their fore fathers.
The legacy of leadership, integrity, courage, strength and
 vigilance
They head their families with love and diligence
Protecting and providing their every need
Because they have been called
Called by their Lord to lead and to love
And to persevere in adversity

Men of Valor
Sometimes they display maternal instincts
And in their weakness we see strength
Because they are an embodiment of power
Men of Valor!
They raise their sons to be men of integrity and dignity
And their sons accept the mantle of manhood with alacrity
Men of Valor, rise run and call all men to carry forth the
 legacy
The legacy of leadership, integrity, courage and vigilance-
Raise your hands if you are a man of valor
We, we salute our men of valor

A Brother's Love So Profound

Every time I turn around
I am surrounded
By a brother's love so profound
At birth he found me
And would never let go
So tiny and small
Yet tough to protect me
A brother's love so profound
He sought only the best for me
He pushed forward for me
When I couldn't push
He fought for me
When I couldn't fight
A brother's love so profound
I look up to
He loves like a father
He protects like a father
He stands in as a father

A brother's love so profound
I would never beg for
A brother's love so profound
I would never let go
Because he would always be there for me
Though separated by life and distance
We are bonded by chords of love

A brother's love so profound
Memories from child hood
We would always share
But the greatest of all
Is a love so profound
That will never fade.

Children

Confidence Selfies

Each morning she took a selfie
A selfie to affirm herself that she was beautiful
Yet the selfies gave her no affirmation
She would take selfies over and over again
Yet the selfies gave her no confirmation-
No confirmation of who she really was
The social media critics who acted like God, judged her
 painfully
But unlike God, whose judgement is compassionate
The social media critics were never compassionate
But little girl look at you
You need no compassionate critics
Because you are unapologetically beautiful
You have been adorned like a peacock
And your beauty radiates from within
You were wonderfully designed by the master of art
Whose artistic work supersedes all the great earthly artists
Like a peacock, walk into that room with confidence
And take the **confidence selfies**
Let the confidence selfies reign
Because there is no other selfie
Like your **confident selfie**!

Words

Words, they make her smile
Words, they make her cry
Words, they uplift her
Words, they bring her down
Words, they inspire her
Words build her confidence
Words mold her into who she will become
Be cautious of the words you use around her.

Oh Daughter so much like me

She was handed over to me wrapped like a burrito
I looked into her eyes
And behold we locked eyes
We gazed at each other as if we had met before
It was love at first sight
I was bewildered by her size and her beauty
Her almond eyes -bold, bright, white
And the prettiest I had ever seen
Eyes so beautiful and very much like mine
Oh wondrous creator, your creation so amazing!
How you created a daughter so much like me is beyond my
imagination
Oh daughter so much like me!
Her little pouty lips just like mine
Couldn't tell me how much she loved me
But every gaze at her beautiful bold eyes, said it all
I could hear "I love you mama" through her eyes
Her soft voice so much like mine
For a moment I thought I was listening to myself
Every single act by my daughter reminds me so much of
myself

Oh daughter so much like me!
Your very presence on earth reminds me
Of a wondrous creator
Who is able to create two similar creations without a blunder
Your very presence on earth reminds me of a creator so
artistic
Oh daughter, stay close to me
Because you are me
And I am you
Daughter love me forever
Because I am you and you are me
Oh daughter so much like me
I would forever hold you close.

Sunshine Son

Sunshine Son
You wake up every morning
With an irresistible smile
A smile that makes it all worth it for mama
Sunshine Son
You will go the extra mile to put a smile on your mama's face
Sunshine Son
Mama adores the deep love you have for her
Your love for mama is immeasurable
And she knows it
The connection between you and mama is unquestionable
Sunshine Son
Your gentility is admired by all
Because in all you do, you stand tall
Sunshine Son
Be Confident in all you do
Never stop dreaming
Let integrity reign in your life
Call on God during hard times
Sunshine Son
You make my life complete
Keep shining, the world needs more Sunshine

For Eryka I cried

I cried when she came running
I cried when she was calling
"Mama! Mama! Mama!"
When horror struck
She had no one to turn to
But Mama
In her little mind
Mama was her only savior
I cried when she came running
Alas! The unthinkable had happened
Alas! Horrendous beyond human imagination
Hair ablaze, hair on fire
She called "Mama! Mama! Mama"
I was all she needed at the time
I cried when she came running
I cried when she was calling
I cried unto my Lord
He was the only one
Who could save my little girl
I cried when he gave me wisdom
I cried because he gave me strength
To save my little girl
The night was long
The wound was deep
I was helpless, he was helpless
But I cried
For Eryka I cried
For Eryka, I will always cry unto my savior

Daddy I Remember

Daddy I remember
When you sang to me a lullaby
From January to December
Your soothing voice
Put me in a peaceful slumber
Daddy I remember
When you urged me on to walk
When I could only crawl
And was too terrified to stand on my feet
Daddy I remember
When you called me your queen
And always treated me like a queen
Though you are not here
I still see myself as a queen
Daddy I remember
When you always whispered in my ears
Each time I left for school
"Fear not! For the Lord is with you"
Though you are not here
I still hear you whisper in my ears
"Fear Not! For the Lord is with you"
When I am too afraid to venture
Daddy I remember
When you wrote letters
When we were apart
Daddy your letters
Inspired and motivated me
To reach the skies

Daddy I remember
When you danced with me
You danced with me
When I was sad
You danced with me
When I was happy
Daddy I remember
When you told me
Life would have been meaningless if I hadn't come along
Daddy I remember
When you helped me choose Mr. Right
He is still right
If you would ask me
Daddy I remember
When you always reminded me of how much
You loved me
Today I am carrying forth
Your love to your grandchildren
I am whispering to them
All the things you whispered
In my ears because
Daddy I remember

Her Love for Daddy

Her father's love
Her first true love
Unaccustomed to the love of another man
She adores him
She clings to him
Like a snail on the wall
And will never let go
Her father's embrace
Is like an eternal wall of protection
Each day he looks into her eyes
He wonders
How an innocent soul
Could be so fond of him
His chest she will forever
Lay her head
Because it is her place of comfort
He would always be her yardstick
To finding her Prince
He will always be her king

Knowing that they are mine forever

In God's eyes he saw
Beyond what I could see
Gave me these precious
Little ones as gifts
I would cherish forever
In God's eyes he saw
Beyond what I could see
And gave me these precious gifts
To love unconditionally
Many days I wondered
Where they came from
Many days I wondered
How they came to be a part of my life forever
Many days I wondered
How my love for them is beyond measure
Many days I worried
When they were away from me
Many days I Prayed
For them to be the best in whatever they did
Many days I prayed
That they would be loved by all mankind
Many days I contemplated
About their future
Many days I battled
On my Knees
Praying that they will make –
The best choices in life

Many days I prayed that
They would always come home
When they are old and married
Many days their ever dependence on me
Made me a better person in life
Today I am grateful
Now and forever
Knowing that they are mine forever

Unspoken Innocence

The unspoken innocence
Though quiet and unspoken
Can be heard in the eyes of that child.
As she dances in the streets
To her own tune
As if no one is watching
We are all smitten by this innocence
And wish we could do same
As we look on we adore her honesty
And bluntness which emanates out of innocence
And we wish we could do same
Her honesty is like a sword
It cuts through the soul
And generates laughter
Which is unparalleled to none other
As we look on we watch in admiration
As she runs in tears to hug the father
Who yelled at her a minute ago
Oh! How quick she is to forgive
Oh! How pleasant the world would be
If we could all do same

Friendhip

Laugh with me Angela

Jingle bells, jingle bells laughing all the way
Angela & Olivia
Laughing about all things, yet laughing about nothing
Angela and Olivia
Talking about all things, yet talking about nothing
Oh how sweet to share the nothingness of life with Angela
and still make it fulfilling.
Angela and Olivia will fulfill the needs of a friend
When life is dull and all is null
Angela and Olivia will fulfill the needs of a friend
By being there and upholding each other
By laughing their way to a strong friendship
My Darling, My friend, I found you because you are right
for my soul
and you fill the nothingness part of my soul by making me
laugh away the worries of life
Laugh with me Angela,
Laugh with me Olivia,
Share your Secrets with me
Bond with me and let's laugh at the nothingness of life.
Jingle bells Jingle Bells laughing all the way.

Loyal Lola

Loyal Lola
I have always wondered
I have always pondered
What the world would be
Without a friend like Loyal Lola
Loyal Lola responds to the call of friendship
Like no other
Her honesty cuts like a knife
But seeks only the best for a friend
Loyal Lola is what the world needs
Loyal Lola will be there to hold my hands through good
times and bad times

Your hands around me

Your hands around me
Is all I need
You make me laugh louder
When I feel like crying louder
You pull me up
When I feel as though I am drowning in my tears
Your hands wrapped around me
Is all I need
Your ears are wide open
When I need a listening ear
When I'm in a state of Melancholy
You hoist my spirit
With your hands wrapped around me
Our dreams are intertwined
Because we share
My trust you have,
Your trust I have
With your hands around me
Till the end of time

About the Author

Olivia Ansa-Sam is a Financial Analyst, an entrepreneur, a Sunday school teacher, a Clothing Designer and a marriage counselor. She hails from the central region of Ghana, West Africa and a product of the University of Ghana where she attained her bachelor's degree in English. Olivia, also holds a diploma in Journalism from the Ghana Institute of Journalism and a Master's degree in Business Administration from University of Maryland University College. She has contributed to her churches Newsletter by writing articles on Marriage and love.

Olivia enjoys writing to inspire and motivate people. She also enjoys reading, sewing, exercising, teaching children at Sunday school, cooking and spending time with her family. She is looking forward to writing more books about Marriage and life lessons to inspire her generation. She currently resides in Maryland with her family.

Final Thought

Dear Reader,

As you read this collection of poems, I want you to meditate on every word and verse. Let the verses speak to you, let the words inspire you to be the best version of yourself. Also know that life is what you make of it .You can choose to fight and achieve your dreams or choose to relinquish. I challenge you today to rise up and face your fears, trust in the Lord to help you fight your battles because you are a conqueror. You have so much power and strength deposited in you more than you can imagine. Remember whatever you are going through now although painful, is sharpening and moulding you to be a stronger version of yourself and also to testify to the goodness of God.

Love with all your heart, let forgiveness reign in your life and remember perseverance will always reap results.

Lastly remember the famous quote "If it must be done, It must be done well" –Unknown

Readers, I employ you to let this be your guiding principles in life and Let God take care of the rest.

Printed in the United States
by Baker & Taylor Publisher Services

Printed in the United States
By Bookmasters